WARREN COUNTY OHIO

Apprenticeship and Indenture Records

1824–1832 and 1864–1867

W. Louis Phillips, C.G.

HERITAGE BOOKS
2010

HERITAGE BOOKS
AN IMPRINT OF HERITAGE BOOKS, INC.

Books, CDs, and more—Worldwide

For our listing of thousands of titles see our website
at
www.HeritageBooks.com

Published 2010 by
HERITAGE BOOKS, INC.
Publishing Division
100 Railroad Ave. #104
Westminster, Maryland 21157

International Standard Book Numbers
Paperbound: 978-1-55613-039-7
Clothbound: 978-0-7884-8553-4

Warren County, Ohio
Apprenticeship & Indenture Records
1824-1832 and 1864-1867

W. Louis Phillips, C.G.*

As can be quickly recognized by examining the following abstracts, indenture or apprenticeship records can be some of the most valuable and informative records ever encountered by the genealogical researcher. It appears that the majority of the children who were being bound out were from poor families, or were without one or both of their parents. In most cases, an accurate date of birth is available for the child, and frequently the name of a parent(s) or guardian is provided along with places of residence.

Any researcher who finds a person of interest in the following abstracts should also examine the actual record in its entirety for more details. As an example, the complete indenture record for Washington Fox Adams (1825) is presented following these introductory comments.

An index to all the indentured children follows the abstracts. Names of parents, guardians, county or township officials, masters and witnesses were not indexed. The indentures appear in this publication as they were found on microfilm at the Ohio Historical Society (GR-5251), which is basically chronological in arrangement.

It is interesting to note that indenture records for approximately the same time period are also available for Preble County (1825-1831). Abstracts of these Preble County indentures were published in "Gateway to the West," 2(3): 112-114(1969). Anyone having knowledge of indenture records for any other county in Ohio is encouraged to contact the author.

An act of the 29th Ohio General Assembly, dated 6 February 1824, entitled "An Act for the Appointment of Guardians," may explain why we find County Recorders recording indentures commencing circa 1824. Section No. 7 of this act pertains specifically to indentures:

"That any guardian or guardians appointed as aforesaid, for any female under the age of twelve, or any male under the age of fourteen years, may, if it be necessary, bind such minor or minors to any suitable person, until such minor or minors, (if a male,) shall arrive at the age of twenty-one years, and if a female, at the age of eighteen years: Provided, that before the indenture whereby any minor or minors may be bound to service, according to this section, shall be holden valid in law, the person or persons to whom such minor or minors shall be bound as aforesaid, and also the terms and covenants in such indenture contained, shall be approved of by the court; and a certificate of the clerk, with the seal of such court, shall be attached to such indenture, in testimony of such approbation."

* W. Louis Phillips, C.G., P.O. Box 24111, Columbus, OH 43224.

Pages 10-12, the indenture for Washington Fox Adams:

This indenture made this 15th day of September in the year
of our Lord one thousand eight hundred and twenty five, wit-
nesseth that Washington Fox Adams, aged fourteen years,
four months and five days, son of the late John Adams
deceased of the County of Warren and State of Ohio, hath of
his own free will and accord, and with the approbation of William McLean his guardian of the County of Miami and State
aforesaid, placed and bound himself an apprentice unto
Thomas Biggs, saddler, of the Town of Lebanon and County of
Warren aforesaid to learn the art, trade, mystery & occupation
of a saddler which he the said Thomas Biggs now useth, and
with him, the said Thomas Biggs, as an apprentice to dwell
and serve for and during the full term of five years, seven
months and twenty five days from the day of the date hereof
during all which said term of five years, seven months &
twenty five days the said Washington doth covenant and
promise to and with the said Thomas that he the said
Washington shall and will, well(?) and faithfully serve and
demean himself, and be just and true to him the said Thomas
as his master and keep his secrets, and every where willingly
obey all his lawful commands.
    That he shall do no hurt or damage to his said master in
his goods, estate or otherwise, nor willingly suffer any to be
done by others & whether presented or not, shall forthwith give
notice thereof to his said master that he shall not inordently
embezle or waste the the goods of said master, nor lend them
without his consent to any person or persons whatsoever, he
shall not traffic or buy and sell with his own goods or the
goods of others during the said term without his masters
leave, he shall not play at cards, dices, or any other unlawful
games, he shall not haunt or frequent play houses or taverns,
or alehouses except it be about his masters business there to
be done, he shall not commit fornication, he shall not contract
matrimony, and he shall not at anytime, by day or night,
depart or absent himself from the service of his said master

v

without his leave, but in all things as a good and faithful apprentice shall and will demean himself to his said master, and all his during the said term.

And the said Thomas Biggs on his part for the consideration of the premises, doth covenant and agree to and with the said guardian and apprentice, each by himself respectively and jointly to teach and instruct the said Washington, or otherwise cause him to be well and sufficiently instructed and taught in the art, trade, mystery and occupation of a saddler after the best way and means he can. And that he the said Thomas will provide for and allow to the said Washington, meat, drink, washing, lodging and apparel for summer and winter and all other necessaries proper and convenient for such an apprentice during the term of his apprenticeship and also teach and instruct him the said apprentice or cause him to be taught and instructed to read, write & cypher through the single rule of three, and in addition to such instruction shall put him said apprentice to some good english school for the full term of nine months, during his said apprenticeship, & which said nine months schooling shall be given to said apprentice during the last three years of his apprenticeship, and before he arrives to the age of twenty years at which age the said term of said apprenticeship will expire, and at the expiration of said term the said Thomas shall and will give unto the said apprentice one Bible and two suits of clothes, one of which shall be worth the sum of forty dollars and the other of common wearing apparel.

In witness whereof the parties have hereunto set their hands & seals the day & year first above written. Signed, sealed & delivered in presence of us,

John Reeves   Washington F. Adams
George Reeves   Wm McLean, gdn
                   Thomas Biggs

Received for record 22 Oct. 1825
Recorded 3 Nov. 1825
A. Brown(?), RWC (recorder, Warren Co.)

Page & date: p. 1   12 July 1824

Indentured: Elizabeth Benham

Age: 13Y 5M 28D

Residence:

Parent, guardian -dau. of Absolom Benham (deceased) & Mary
or officials: his widow

Residence:

Bound to: David & Eliz. Baker   Trade: housewifery

Residence:

Term: 4Y 6M 2D until 18 on 21 Dec 1828 (birthday)

Witnesses: George Johnson, Sr. & Manuel Heath

Page & date: pp. 2-3   8 Nov 1824

Indentured: Vesey or Veazey Bunnel

Age: 16Y 3M 17D

Residence:

Parent, guardian -George Lowery or Lowry, gdn
or officials:

Residence: Clear Creek Twp., WR Co.

Bound to: Manlove Reed   Trade: cabinet maker

Residence: Clear Creek Twp., WR Co.

Term: 4Y 9M 13D until 21 on 21 June 1829 (birthday)

Witnesses: Wm Newport & James E. Dearth, J.P.

Page & date: pp. 4-5   no date (1824); recorded 20 Jan 1825

Indentured: William Denny

Age: 14Y

Residence: Lebanon, OH

Parent, guardian -James Birdsall, gdn.; both parents dead
or officials:

Residence:

Bound to: William Sellers   Trade: printing

Residence:

Term: 7 years from this date until 21 on 4 Dec 1831

Witnesses: P. DeWandelaer(?) & James Fife

WARREN COUNTY, OHIO APPRENTICESHIP & INDENTURE RECORDS

Page & date:	pp. 5-6 4 Jan 1825
Indentured:	Nancy Ann Daughterty, a poor girl
Age:	5Y 1M 19D
Residence:	probably Wayne Twp., WR Co.
Parent, guardian or officials:	-dau. of Elizabeth Daughterty; trustees of Wayne Twp.: John Satterthwaite, J.P., Frederick
Residence:	Stanton & Joseph White
Bound to:	Rachel Evans Trade: housewifery
Residence:	Wayne Twp.
Term:	12Y 10M 11D until 18 on 16 Nov 1837
Witnesses:	Jesse Ware & Morgan Folkerson

Page & date:	pp. 7-8 4 Jan 1825
Indentured:	Precious Daugherty, a poor girl
Age:	3Y 49D
Residence:	probably Wayne Twp.
Parent, guardian or officials:	-dau. of Elizabeth Daugherty; same officials as above
Residence:	
Bound to:	Rachel Evans Trade: housewifery
Residence:	Wayne Twp.
Term:	14Y 316D until 18 on 16 Nov 1839
Witnesses:	Jesse Ware & Morgan Fulkerson

Page & date:	pp. 8-9 16 Oct 1824
Indentured:	George Washington Woodington, a destitute child and not provided for by his father
Age:	11Y 10M 20D
Residence:	probably Turtle Creek Twp.
Parent, guardian or officials:	-son of John Woodington; trustees of Turtle Creek Twp.: Patrick Meloy, James Cowan, Jr. & John Reeves; John M. Houston, J.P.
Residence:	
Bound to:	Josiah Townsend Trade: blacksmithing
Residence:	WR Co.
Term:	9Y 1M 11D until 21 on 27 Nov 1833
Witnesses:	Jeremiah Smith & An'ty Geoghegan

Page & date: pp. 9-10   12 Mar 1825

Indentured: Emanuel Heath

Age: 18Y 2M 20D

Residence:

Parent, guardian   -son of Mary Heath, his father being deceased
or officials:

Residence:

Bound to: David Baker   Trade: tayloring

Residence:

Term: 2Y 9M 11D until 21 on 23 Dec 1827

Witnesses: James Grimes & Eleazer Coffeen

Page & date: pp. 10-12   15 Sep 1825

Indentured: Washington Fox Adams

Age: 14Y 4M 5D

Residence:

Parent, guardian   - son of the late John Adams of WR Co.
or officials: Wm McLean of Miami Co., OH his gdn

Residence:

Bound to: Thomas Biggs   Trade: saddler

Residence: Lebanon, OH

Term: 5Y 7M 25 D until 20

Witnesses: John Reeves & George Reeves

Page & date: pp. 12-13   27 Aug 1825

Indentured: Grizzy Lindey or Lindsey, a girl

Age: 10Y 2M 20D

Residence:

Parent, guardian   -dau. of Oliver Lindey who is absent;
or officials: Trustees of Union Twp.: John M. Snook & John
                    Hall; Henry Foster, J.P.
Residence:

Bound to: Isaac Stubbs   Trade:

Residence: Union Twp., WR Co.

Term: 7Y 9M 10D until 18 on 7 June 1833

Witnesses: Calvin Muntague & John Phillips

Page & date:	p. 14 21 Nov 1825
Indentured:	John Hill, Jr.
Age:	12Y 4M 24D
Residence:	Lemon Twp., Butler Co., OH
Parent, guardian or officials:	son of John Hill
Residence:	Lemon Twp., Butler Co., OH
Bound to:	James Sweney or Sweny Trade: carpenter
Residence:	Clearcreek Twp., WR Co.
Term:	8Y 7M 7D until 21 on 27 June 1834
Witnesses:	George Riddell & John M. Houston

Page & date:	pp. 15-16 27 Jan 1826
Indentured:	John Tullis
Age:	15Y 9M 26D
Residence:	
Parent, guardian or officials:	-with consent of his gdn, David Tullis
Residence:	
Bound to:	Wm Russel, Jr. Trade: clothier
Residence:	
Term:	5Y 2M 4D until 21 on 1 Apr 1831
Witnesses:	J. M. Houston

Page & date:	pp. 16-17 14 Apr 1826
Indentured:	William Farris (see also p.53 for void of this indenture)
Age:	13Y 8M 2D
Residence:	Washington Twp., WR Co.
Parent, guardian or officials:	with consent of gdn, Robert L. Jack
Residence:	
Bound to:	George F. Longstreth Trade: farming (or Longsheth)
Residence:	WR Co.
Term:	7Y 3M 29D until 21 on 12 Aug 1833
Witnesses:	John M. Houston

Page & date:	pp. 17-19 25 May 1826
Indentured:	Ann Kinney, a poor & destitute child whose parents have gone to places unknown to us
Age:	7Y 8M from the best information we have
Residence:	probably Turtle Creek Twp., WR Co.
Parent, guardian or officials:	-Trustees of Turtle Creek Twp.: Ichabod Corwin, James Cowan, Jr. & John Reeves; John M. Houston, J.P.
Residence:	
Bound to:	Daniel Voorhis Trade: servant
Residence:	Turtle Creek Twp.
Term:	10Y 4M until 18 on or about 25 Sep 1836
Witnesses:	William Frost & McLean Blair

Page & date:	pp. 19-20 25 May 1826
Indentured:	William Vansickel, a poor boy
Age:	11Y 9M as is supposed
Residence:	probably Turtle Creek Twp., WR Co.
Parent, guardian or officials:	- same officials as above parents are deceased, names unknown
Residence:	
Bound to:	John Mounts Trade: coopering
Residence:	Turtle Creek Twp.
Term:	9Y 3M until 21 on or about 25 Aug 1835
Witnesses:	William Frost & McLean Blair

Page & date:	pp. 20-22 15 Apr 1826
Indentured:	William Henry Emrey, a poor child
Age:	none given
Residence:	probably Washington Twp., WR Co.
Parent, guardian or officials:	-John L. Williams & Christy McCray, overseers of the poor of Wash. Twp.; Wm Wilkerson, J.P.
Residence:	
Bound to:	William H. Robertson Trade: farmer
Residence:	Wash. Twp.
Term:	until 21 on 21 Feb 1840
Witnesses:	Thos Jones

WARREN COUNTY, OHIO APPRENTICESHIP & INDENTURE RECORDS

Page & date: pp. 22-23   8 Aug 1826

Indentured: Moses McPheeters or McPheters or McPeeters

Age: 14Y 5M 23D

Residence:

Parent, guardian   -son of Moses McPheeters, Sr.
or officials:

Residence:

Bound to: David Baker   Trade: Taylor

Residence:

Term: 5Y 7M 24D until aged 21Y 1M 16D; birthday is
Witnesses: 1 Apr
     Manuel Heath & William Zigman(?)

Page & date: pp. 23-24   12 Aug 1826

Indentured: Veazey Bunnell

Age: 18Y 1M 12D

Residence:

Parent, guardian   -George Lowry, gdn
or officials:

Residence:

Bound to: Wm M. Wiles   Trade: cabinet maker

Residence: Lebanon

Term: 2Y 9M 19D until 21 on 30 June 1829

Witnesses: John M. Houston

Page & date: pp. 24-25   23 Aug 1826

Indentured: George Matthews

Age: 16Y 3M 27D

Residence:

Parent, guardian   -son of James Matthews
or officials:

Residence: WR Co.

Bound to: Benj Kemp   Trade: taylor

Residence: Wayne Twp.

Term: until 21 on 26 Apr 1831

Witnesses: George C. Ward & Sarah Ward

Page & date: pp. 25-27   26 July 1826

Indentured: David Snider or Snyder

Age: 17Y 5M 28D

Residence: WR Co.

Parent, guardian   -son of John Snider/Snyder
or officials:

Residence: WR Co. (twp. not legible)

Bound to: William Williason   Trade: weaving

Residence: Hamilton Twp.

Term: until 21 on 29 Jan. 1830; 3Y 6M 3D

Witnesses: John Snyder & Joab Snook

Page & date: pp. 27-28   14 Oct 1826

Indentured: Warren Anderson

Age: 17Y 2M 4D

Residence:

Parent, guardian   -with consent of gdn, David Coddington
or officials:

Residence:

Bound to: Adam Koogle   Trade: hatter

Residence: Lebanon

Term: 3Y 9M 24D until 21 on 10 Aug 1830

Witnesses: J. M. Houston

Page & date: pp. 28-29   22 Sep 1826

Indentured: Jesse Clegg

Age: 14Y 6M

Residence: WR Co.

Parent, guardian   -son of Richard Clegg
or officials:

Residence: WR Co.

Bound to: John Morford   Trade: potter

Residence: WR Co.

Term: until 22 Mar 1833 upon 21st birthday

Witnesses: Jacob Pearson & Lewis Lewis

Page & date: pp. 30-31   23 Sep 1826

Indentured: William Cowgill

Age: 15Y 4M 3D

Residence:

Parent, guardian -son of Phebe Cowgill; father deceased
or officials:

Residence:

Bound to: Joseph J. Johnson   Trade: saddler

Residence: WR Co.

Term: 5Y 7M 26D until 21 on 18 May 1832

Witnesses: George J. Cowgill, John W. Cowgill & Wm Gutery

Page & date: pp. 31-32   8 Dec 1826

Indentured: Charles Blake

Age: 13Y 1M 17D

Residence: WR Co.

Parent, guardian -son of Samuel Blake
or officials:

Residence: WR Co.

Bound to: Jarvis Stokes   Trade: farmer

Residence: WR Co.

Term: until 21 on 19 Oct 1834

Witnesses: John Satterthwaite & Charles Hockins

Page & date: pp. 33-34   23 Oct 1826

Indentured: Henry Fulks, a poor boy

Age: 1Y 10M 11D

Residence: Hamilton Twp.

Parent, guardian -son of Polly Fulks who is unable to support her
or officials: said child; John Snook & James Kelly, overseers of
Residence: the poor of Hamilton Twp.; Robert Wilson, J.P.

Bound to: Ephraim Drake   Trade: farming & common
Residence: Union Twp.   shoemaking

Term: 19Y 1M 19D until 21 on 12 Dec 1845

Witnesses: Owen Legg & Nathan K. Snook

Page & date: pp. 35-36   22 Nov 1826

Indentured: Latitia Runyan, an illegitimate dau. of Sarah
                  Farquer
Age: 6Y 3M ? D

Residence: Hamilton Twp.

Parent, guardian -see above
or officials:

Residence: Hamilton Twp.

Bound to: James Stryker   Trade: housewifery

Residence: Hamilton Twp.

Term: 11Y 8M 20D until 18 on 12 Aug 1838

Witnesses: Robert Wilson &Jeptha Bitchy

Page & date: pp. 36-37   29 Dec 1826

Indentured: Sally Ann Love

Age: 7Y 6D

Residence: Washington Twp.

Parent, guardian -Christie/Christy McCray & John L. Williams,
or officials: overseers of the poor; Samuel Bowman, J.P.

Residence: Washington Twp.

Bound to: Wm Wilkerson   Trade: housekeeping

Residence: Washington Twp.

Term: until 18 on 23 Dec 1837

Witnesses: Robert E. Vandoren & David Vanshoyck

Page & date: pp. 37-39   25 Nov 1826

Indentured: Samuel Myers, a poor boy

Age: 5Y 8M 21D

Residence: probably Wayne Twp.

Parent, guardian -Joseph White & David Evans, overseers of the poor;
or officials: John Satterthwaite, J.P

Residence: Wayne Twp.

Bound to: Edward L. Kenrick   Trade: farmer

Residence: WR Co.

Term: until 21 on 4 Mar 1842

Witnesses: Sarah Ward & George C. Ward

Page & date: pp. 39-40   29 Dec 1826

Indentured: <u>Purnall/Purnal Stewart</u>

Age: 16Y 8M 20D

Residence: Greene Co., OH

Parent, guardian - son of William Stewart
or officials:

Residence: Greene Co.

Bound to: Benj. Kemp   Trade: taylor

Residence: WR Co.

Term: until 21 on 9 Apr 1831

Witnesses: Sarah & George C. Ward

Page & date: pp. 40-41   31 Jan 1827

Indentured: <u>Meekley Jones</u> (or Meekly)

Age: 5Y 9M 21D

Residence: Wayne Twp.

Parent, guardian -son of George Jones, absconded; Joseph White &
or officials: David Evans, overseers of the poor; John Satter-
Residence: thwaite, J.P. - all of Wayne Twp.

Bound to: Nathan Dicks   Trade: farming

Residence: Wayne Twp.

Term: 15Y 2M 10D until 21

Witnesses: George C. Ward & Jos B. Chapman

Page & date: pp. 41-42   12 Feb 1827

Indentured: <u>William Sagers</u>

Age: 11Y 9M 5D

Residence: Wayne Twp.

Parent, guardian -son of Mary Davies
or officials:

Residence: Wayne Twp.

Bound to: John Emly   Trade: farmer

Residence: Wayne Twp.

Term: until 21 on 7 May 1836

Witnesses: George C. & Sarah Ward

WARREN COUNTY, OHIO APPRENTICESHIP & INDENTURE RECORDS

Page & date: pp. 42-43   20 Jan 1827

Indentured: Mary McFadgen, a poor girl

Age: 13Y on 20 June last

Residence: Salem Twp.

Parent, guardian   -Wm Armstrong, Mahlon Roach & George B. Whitacre
or officials: Salem Twp. Trustees; Benj. Baldwin, J.P.

Residence:

Bound to: Andrew Lytle   Trade: housewifery

Residence:

Term: until 18

Witnesses: Thomas Adams & William B. Lytle

Page & date: pp. 43-45   20 Jan 1827

Indentured: Cornelius McFadgen, a poor boy

Age: 13Y on 20 June last

Residence: Salem Twp.

Parent, guardian   -same officials as above
or officials:

Residence: Salem Twp.

Bound to: Andrew Lytle   Trade: tanning & curying

Residence:

Term: until 21

Witnesses: Thomas Adams & William B. Lytle

Page & date: pp. 45-46   12 May 1827

Indentured: David Harvy or Harvey

Age: 11Y on 4 July next

Residence: WR Co.

Parent, guardian   -son of John Harvy or Harvey
or officials:

Residence: WR Co.

Bound to: Solomon Fry or Frey   Trade: house carpenter
                                             & cabinet maker
Residence:

Term: until 21 on 4 July 1837

Witnesses: Daniel Crane & Henry Joseph Frey

WARREN COUNTY, OHIO APPRENTICESHIP & INDENTURE RECORDS

Page & date: pp. 46-48   12 May 1827
Indentured: Felix Harvy or Harvey
Age: 7Y on 18 Apr last
Residence: WR Co.
Parent, guardian -son of John Harvy or Harvey
or officials:
Residence: WR Co.
Bound to: Christian or Christopher   Trade: husbandry
Residence: Fry
Term: until 18 on 18 Apr 1838
Witnesses: Henry Joseph Frey & Daniel Crane

Page & date: pp. 48-49   29 May 1827
Indentured: John Wood
Age: 15Y 2M 15D
Residence: Turtlecreek Twp.
Parent, guardian -son of Aquilles Wood
or officials:
Residence: Turtlecreek Twp.
Bound to: Anthony Warwick   Trade: blacksmith
Residence: Turtlecreek Twp.
Term: until 21 on 14 Mar 1833; 5Y 9M 15D
Witnesses: Saml Chamberlin & Lewis Chamberlin

Page & date: pp. 50-51   23 July 1827
Indentured: Robert Taylor Foster
Age: 14Y 22D
Residence:
Parent, guardian -son of Nathaniel Foster deceased; with consent of
or officials: his mother, Catherine Foster
Residence:
Bound to: Anthony Warwick   Trade: blacksmith
Residence: WR Co.
Term: until 21 on 1 July 1833; 6Y 11M 9D
Witnesses: Saml Chamberlin & Lewis Chamberlin

WARREN COUNTY, OHIO APPRENTICESHIP & INDENTURE RECORDS

Page & date:	pp. 51-52 9 Oct 1827
Indentured:	Mary An Gordan, a poor girl
Age:	14Y 7M 5D
Residence:	Washington Twp.
Parent, guardian or officials:	-John L. Williams & George F. Longstreth, overseers of the poor; Wm Wilkerson, J.P.
Residence:	Washington Twp.
Bound to:	Joel Drake Trade: housewifery
Residence:	Washington Twp.
Term:	until 18; born 4 Mar 1813
Witnesses:	Wm T. Jones & Wm Wilkerson

Page & date:	p. 53 15 Nov 1827
Indentured:	William Farris - previous indenture being voided see pp. 16-17
Age:	
Residence:	
Parent, guardian or officials:	-Wm arrived at age 14 and chose Thomas Courl of Clark Co. to be his gdn. via Court of Common Pleas of Clark Co. Indenture with Longstreth voided.
Residence:	
Bound to:	George F. Longstreth Trade:
Residence:	
Term:	
Witnesses:	J. M. Houston

Page & date:	pp. 53-55 20 Nov 1827
Indentured:	Jepthal Ritchey
Age:	15Y 8M 4D
Residence:	Hamilton Twp.
Parent, guardian or officials:	-son of Robert Ritchey
Residence:	Hamilton Twp.
Bound to:	David Baker Trade: taylor
Residence:	Lebanon
Term:	until 21 on 16 Mar 1833; 5Y 3M 27D
Witnesses:	John M. Houston

Page & date:	pp. 55-57 20 Feb 1828
Indentured:	**Parnell or Purnel Stewart**
Age:	17Y 10M 11D
Residence:	WR Co.
Parent, guardian or officials:	-son of William Stewart
Residence:	WR Co.
Bound to:	Job Barton Trade: taylor
Residence:	Wayne Twp.
Term:	until 21 on 9 Apr 1831
Witnesses:	Hugh Shotwell & George C. Ward

Page & date:	pp. 57-58 9 Feb 1828
Indentured:	**Isaac H. Roll**
Age:	16Y 1M 27D
Residence:	Lebanon
Parent, guardian or officials:	-son of Joseph Roll
Residence:	Lebanon
Bound to:	James McFisher Trade: saddle & harness
Residence:	making
Term:	until aged 20Y 7M 18D; 4Y 5M 22D; 1 Aug 1832
Witnesses:	Joseph J. Johnson

Page & date:	pp. 58-60 18 Feb 1828
Indentured:	**John Rodgers**
Age:	15Y 5M 10D
Residence:	Turtlecreek Twp.
Parent, guardian or officials:	-son of Edward Rodgers
Residence:	Turtlecreek Twp.
Bound to:	Asbury Frazier Trade: taylor & habit
Residence:	Lebanon maker
Term:	until 21 on 8 Sep 1833; 5Y 6M 21D
Witnesses:	none

Page & date:	pp. 60-62 17 Apr 1828
Indentured:	Catherine McKnight
Age:	10Y 5M 7D
Residence:	WR Co.
Parent, guardian or officials:	-minor heir at law of Wm McKnight, late of WR Co. Lewis David, gdn.
Residence:	
Bound to:	Daniel & Eleanor Stoutenburough Trade: housewifery
Residence:	WR Co.
Term:	until 18 on 10 Nov 1835
Witnesses:	J. K. Wilds & John M. Williams

Page & date:	pp. 62-64 3 May 1828
Indentured:	Jane Stevens (see also p.104 for void of this indenture)
Age:	3Y 7M
Residence:	
Parent, guardian or officials:	-dau. of George Stevens
Residence:	
Bound to:	Jesse & Nancy Newport Trade: housewifery
Residence:	
Term:	14Y 5M until 18 on 3 Oct 1845
Witnesses:	J. M. Houston & John Probasco

Page & date:	pp. 64-65 7 June 1828
Indentured:	Lemuel Holland
Age:	17Y 7M 10D
Residence:	WR Co.
Parent, guardian or officials:	-son of James Holland
Residence:	WR Co.
Bound to:	Wm M. Wiles Trade: cabinet making
Residence:	Lebanon
Term:	until 21 on 28 Oct 1831
Witnesses:	George J. Smith & Abraham Delavere(?)

Page & date:	pp. 65-67 14 Apr 1828
Indentured:	Benj. Ely
Age:	18Y 6M 26D
Residence:	
Parent, guardian or officials:	-son of Robert Ely
Residence:	
Bound to:	Joel Satterthwaite Trade: wagon maker
Residence:	WR Co.
Term:	until 21 on 19 Sep 1831
Witnesses:	George C. Ward & Wm Ely

Page & date:	pp. 67-68 1 May 1828
Indentured:	John Hand
Age:	18Y 7M
Residence:	Greene Co., OH
Parent, guardian or officials:	-son of Phebe Ann Hand
Residence:	Greene Co.
Bound to:	Joel Satterthwaite Trade: waggon maker
Residence:	WR Co.
Term:	until 21 on 1 Oct 1830
Witnesses:	Joseph Hawkins & Thomas Ridge

Page & date:	pp. 69-70 15 Apr 1828
Indentured:	Thomas Seaman
Age:	14Y 6M 16D
Residence:	
Parent, guardian or officials:	-Samuel Nixon, gdn
Residence:	
Bound to:	Francis Dill & Lewis Trade: tanner & currier
	Osborn
Residence:	
Term:	until 21 on 29 sep 1834; 6Y 5M 14D
Witnesses:	none

Page & date:	pp. 70-72 16 Aug 1828
Indentured:	David Hopkins
Age:	16Y
Residence:	
Parent, guardian or officials:	-William Hopkins, gdn
Residence:	
Bound to:	Lewis S. Ingersall Trade: tayloring
Residence:	Lebanon
Term:	until 6 Feb 1833 when aged 20Y 9M
Witnesses:	Wm Sellers

Page & date:	pp. 72-73 27 Aug 1828
Indentured:	Orange V. Lemon or Lemen
Age:	15Y 7M
Residence:	WR Co.
Parent, guardian or officials:	-John Reeves, gdn
Residence:	WR Co.
Bound to:	Samuel Nixon Trade: tanning
Residence:	Lebanon
Term:	until 27 Aug 1831 when aged 18 & 7/12 years
Witnesses:	J. M. Houston

Page & date:	pp. 73-75 25 Jan 1827
Indentured:	Aron Robbins
Age:	11Y on the 25 Jan. 1827
Residence:	WR Co.
Parent, guardian or officials:	-son of Timothy Robbins
Residence:	WR Co.
Bound to:	Derrick Barkalow Trade: farmer
Residence:	WR Co.
Term:	until 21 on 25 Jan 1837
Witnesses:	John Cox & Arthur Cox

WARREN COUNTY, OHIO APPRENTICESHIP & INDENTURE RECORDS

Page & date: pp. 75-77   30 Aug 1828

Indentured: John Myers, a pauper

Age: 5Y 5M 22D

Residence: probably Wayne Twp.

Parent, guardian   -Thomas Smith & Micajah Johnson, overseers of the
or officials: poor of Wayne Twp.; Burwell Goode, J.P.

Residence:

Bound to: Wm Antrim or Antram   Trade: farmer

Residence: WR Co.

Term: until 21 on 8 Mar 1844

Witnesses: Joshua Ward & George C. Ward

Page & date: pp. 77-78   27 Nov 1828

Indentured: Michael Davis, an orphan destitute of parents or
                         guardian
Age: 17Y 5M 25D

Residence: probably Turtlecreek Twp.

Parent, guardian   - James Cowan, Jr, Peter Carson & J. M. Houston,
or officials: Trustees of Turtlecreek Twp.; Wm Sellers, J.P.

Residence:

Bound to: Wm M. Wiles   Trade: cabinet making

Residence: Lebanon

Term: 3Y 6M 5D until 21 on 2 June 1832

Witnesses: Nathan Richardson

Page & date: pp. 78-80   8 Oct 1828

Indentured: Robert Hamilton

Age: 17Y 11M 17D

Residence:

Parent, guardian   -John T. Jack, gdn
or officials:

Residence:

Bound to: Henry B. Miller   Trade: cabinet making

Residence: Lebanon

Term: until 21 on 22 Oct 1831

Witnesses: Robt. Hamilton & James D. Courey(?)

Page & date: pp. 80-81   7 May 1828

Indentured: Thomas Stevens

Age: 9Y 4M 29D

Residence:

Parent, guardian -son of George Stevens
or officials:

Residence:

Bound to: John Lewis   Trade: cabinet making

Residence: WR Co.

Term: until 21 on 9 May 1840

Witnesses: J. M. Houston & Geo. Stevens & Paul Lewis, Jr.

Page & date: pp. 81-83   no date, received for record
                                 24 Jan. 1829
Indentured: Nathan Brown

Age: 15Y 10M 16D

Residence: probably Greene Co.

Parent, guardian -step son of Margaret Brown; Ner(?) Haines &
or officials: Micajah Johnson, Trustees

Residence: Greene Co.

Bound to: Thomas Hartly   Trade: blacksmith

Residence: WR Co.

Term: until 21 on 4 July 1833

Witnesses: Wm H. Hartley

Page & date: pp. 83-84   2 Feb 1829

Indentured: Benj. F. Webber, Jr.

Age: 13Y 1M 20D

Residence: Lebanon

Parent, guardian -son of Benj. Webber
or officials:

Residence: Lebanon

Bound to: Samuel Chamberlin   Trade: waggon making

Residence: Lebanon

Term: until 21 on 13 Dec. 1836

Witnesses: Wm Alloways & Lewis Chamberlin

Page & date:	pp. 85-86 3 Jan. 1829
Indentured:	Andrew McIlvaine or McIlvain
Age:	17Y 2M 27D
Residence:	probably Turtlecreek Twp.
Parent, guardian or officials:	-son of Moses McIlvaine, now deceased & having neither parent nor gdn living; Peter Carson & John M. Houston, Trustees - Turtlecreek Twp.; Wm Sellers, J.P.
Residence:	
Bound to:	Henry B. Miller Trade: cabinet making
Residence:	Lebanon
Term:	3Y 9M 1D until 21 on 7 Oct 1832
Witnesses:	none

Page & date:	pp. 86-87 10 Feb 1829
Indentured:	Charles Webber
Age:	11Y 1M
Residence:	Lebanon
Parent, guardian or officials:	-son of Benj. Webber
Residence:	Lebanon
Bound to:	Peter Probasco Trade: plane making
Residence:	Lebanon
Term:	until 21 on 11 Jan. 1839
Witnesses:	Asahel Brown & Henry Brown

Page & date:	pp. 88-89 7 Feb 1829
Indentured:	David Irwin
Age:	18Y 10M 20D
Residence:	WR Co.
Parent, guardian or officials:	-bound himself
Residence:	
Bound to:	Joseph Hartley Trade: blacksmith
Residence:	WR Co.
Term:	until 21 on 17 Mar 1831
Witnesses:	George C. & Mary Ward

WARREN COUNTY, OHIO APPRENTICESHIP & INDENTURE RECORDS

Page & date: pp. 89-91   26 Feb 1829
Indentured: Alexander Hamilton
Age: 16Y 4M 15D
Residence:
Parent, guardian -bound himself with consent of gdn, John T. Jack
or officials:
Residence:
Bound to: Wm M. Wiles   Trade: cabinet making
Residence: Lebanon
Term: 4Y 7M 15D; until 21 on 11 Oct 1833
Witnesses: McLean J. Blair

Page & date: pp. 91-92   26 Jan 1829
Indentured: Wm M. Carter
Age: 12Y 2M 27D
Residence: WR Co.
Parent, guardian - ward of John James
or officials:
Residence: WR Co.
Bound to: Francis B. Howell   Trade: paper making
Residence: WR Co.
Term: until 21 on 30 Oct 1837
Witnesses: John M. Seely

Page & date: pp. 93-94   26 Jan. 1829
Indentured: John Flinn
Age: 14Y 7M 21D
Residence: WR Co.
Parent, guardian -ward of Zepheniah Lee
or officials:
Residence: WR Co.
Bound to: Francis B. Howell   Trade: paper making
Residence: WR Co.
Term: until 21 on 5 June 1835
Witnesses: John M. Seely

Page & date:	pp. 94-96 26 Jan 1829
Indentured:	John Hinkly
Age:	17Y 5M 26D
Residence:	WR Co.
Parent, guardian or officials:	-ward of John James
Residence:	WR Co.
Bound to:	Francis B. Howell Trade: paper making
Residence:	WR Co.
Term:	until 21 on 28 July 1832
Witnesses:	John M. Seely

Page & date:	pp. 96-98 26 Jan 1829
Indentured:	Ebenezer Hinkly
Age:	15Y 6M 18D
Residence:	WR Co.
Parent, guardian or officials:	-ward of John Dunn
Residence:	WR Co.
Bound to:	Francis B. Howell Trade: paper making
Residence:	WR Co.
Term:	until 21 on 8 July 1834
Witnesses:	John M. Seely

Page & date:	pp. 98-99 28 Mar 1829
Indentured:	Milton Vansickles, an orphan destitute child
Age:	having neither father, mother, nor gdn supposed to be about 4Y on the 7 Feb 1829
Residence:	
Parent, guardian or officials:	- Trustees of Turtlecreek Twp.: J. M. Houston & Peter Carson; Jeremiah Smith, J.P.
Residence:	
Bound to:	Amos Thatcher Trade: farming
Residence:	
Term:	until 16 on 7 Feb 1841
Witnesses:	none

Page & date:	pp. 99 - 100 25 Mar 1829
Indentured:	Allen Anderson
Age:	16Y 9M 3D
Residence:	WR Co.
Parent, guardian or officials:	-son of Elizabeth Maloy, formerly Elizabeth Anderson
Residence:	WR Co.
Bound to:	Jacob Eckman Trade: blacksmith
Residence:	WR Co.
Term:	4Y 2M 27D
Witnesses:	A. Tullis & John Hayes

Page & date:	pp. 101-102 9 Feb 1829
Indentured:	Palser B. Bush
Age:	6Y 2M 23D
Residence:	Salem Twp.
Parent, guardian or officials:	-son of William Bush
Residence:	Salem Twp.
Bound to:	Elisha Barber Trade: farming
Residence:	Salem Twp.
Term:	until 21 on 16 Nov 1843; 14Y 9M 7D
Witnesses:	William Crosson & Joseph Homes

Page & date:	pp. 102-104 12 Mar 1829
Indentured:	John Anisman(?) or Arvisman(?)
Age:	15Y 11M 12D
Residence:	
Parent, guardian or officials:	-ward of William H. Hamilton
Residence:	
Bound to:	Francis B. Howell Trade: paper making
Residence:	WR Co.
Term:	until 21 on 21 Mar 1834
Witnesses:	John M. Seely

Page & date:	pp. 104-105 11 Feb 1829
Indentured:	Jane Stevens - previous indenture being voided
Age:	see pp. 62-64
Residence:	
Parent, guardian or officials:	-dau. of George Stevens
Residence:	
Bound to:	Jesse & Nancy Newport Trade:
Residence:	
Term:	
Witnesses:	Thomas Clayton & George Luther

Page & date:	pp. 105-106 18 May 1829
Indentured:	Thomas Morrow
Age:	16Y 1M
Residence:	Lebanon
Parent, guardian or officials:	-son of Alexander Morrow
Residence:	Lebanon
Bound to:	James Longshore Trade: carpenter
Residence:	Lebanon
Term:	until 21 on 18 Apr 1834; 4Y 11M
Witnesses:	John Pauly(?) & Benj. Bright

Page & date:	pp. 106-108 2 Mar 1829
Indentured:	Elizabeth Job
Age:	none given
Residence:	
Parent, guardian or officials:	-dau. of James Job; Christies/Christy McCray, & Wm H. Robinson/Robertson, overseers of the poor of Washington Twp.; Wm Wilkerson, J.P.
Residence:	
Bound to:	Chordy/Chorde Drake Trade: housewifery
Residence:	Washington Twp.
Term:	until 18 on 1 Oct 1841
Witnesses:	Jno. L. Williams

Page & date:	pp. 108-109 10 June 1829
Indentured:	Isaac Ivins(?) Davies (3 names) -surname possibly
Age:	9Y 9M 14D Davis? see below
Residence:	probably Wayne Twp.
Parent, guardian or officials:	-Burwell Goode & Micajah Johnson, overseers of the poor of Wayne Twp.; John Satterthwaite, J.P.
Residence:	
Bound to:	Benj. Kemp Trade: taylor
Residence:	WR Co.
Term:	until 21 on 24 Aug 1840
Witnesses:	George C. Ward & John Satterthwaite, J.P.

Page & date:	pp. 110-111 10 June 1829
Indentured:	John Davis, a poor child -surname possibly Davies?
Age:	7Y 8M 29D
Residence:	probably Wayne Twp.
Parent, guardian or officials:	-same officials as above
Residence:	probably Wayne Twp.
Bound to:	Jason Evans Trade: farmer
Residence:	WR Co.
Term:	until 21 on 12 Sep 1842
Witnesses:	George C. Ward & Benj. Kemp & John Satterthwaite

Page & date:	pp. 111-113 10 June 1829
Indentured:	Rachel Davies, a poor child
Age:	11Y 7M 27D
Residence:	probably Wayne Twp.
Parent, guardian or officials:	-same officials as above
Residence:	
Bound to:	John Emiley Trade: housewifery
Residence:	WR Co.
Term:	until 18 on 14 Oct 1835
Witnesses:	George C. Ward, Jason Evans & John Satterthwaite

Page & date: pp. 113-114   24 June 1829

Indentured: Francis Whitacre - see also p. 127 for void
Age: 14Y   of this indenture

Residence: WR Co.

Parent, guardian   -ward of Samuel Nixon
or officials:

Residence: WR Co.

Bound to: James M. Fisher   Trade: saddle & harnis
Residence: Lebanon   making

Term: until 21 on 24 June 1836

Witnesses: James B. Hays

Page & date: pp. 115-116   9 May 1829

Indentured: Joseph Crossley

Age: 15Y 7M 15D

Residence: WR Co.

Parent, guardian   -son of Charles Crossley
or officials:

Residence: WR Co.

Bound to: Joel Satterthwaite   Trade: waggon maker

Residence: WR Co.

Term: until 21 on 24 Sep. 1834

Witnesses: Jos Hollingsworth & George C. Ward

Page & date: pp. 116-117   7 Aug 1829

Indentured: Samuel Ross

Age: none given

Residence: WR Co.

Parent, guardian   -son of Enoch A. Ross
or officials:

Residence: WR Co.

Bound to: Jesse Helmick   Trade: blacksmith

Residence:

Term: until 21 on 20 Mar 1836

Witnesses: Morlen Tooley

Page & date:	p. 118 3 Sep 1829
Indentured:	Isaac N. Ross
Age:	none given
Residence:	WR Co.
Parent, guardian or officials:	-son of Enoch A. Ross
Residence:	WR Co.
Bound to:	John Hill Trade: none mentioned
Residence:	probably tanning & currying -see below
Term:	until 17 on 7 Oct 1833
Witnesses:	Wm Crosson & David Ross

Page & date:	pp. 118-119 20 July 1829
Indentured:	Moses Ross
Age:	none given
Residence:	WR Co.
Parent, guardian or officials:	-son of Enoch A. Ross
Residence:	WR Co.
Bound to:	John Hill Trade: tanning & currying
Residence:	
Term:	until 21 on 16 Dec 1832
Witnesses:	Nathan Helmick & David Ross

Page & date:	pp. 120-121 3 Sep 1829
Indentured:	Almira Ross
Age:	none given
Residence:	
Parent, guardian or officials:	-dau. of Enoch A. Ross
Residence:	
Bound to:	John & Levina Hill Trade: housewifery
Residence:	
Term:	until 18 on 6 Apr 1843
Witnesses:	Wm Crosson & David Ross

Page & date:	pp. 121-123 26 Aug 1829
Indentured:	David H. Tullis
Age:	17Y on 15 Sep next
Residence:	
Parent, guardian or officials:	-son of the late Jonathan Tullis; Francis Dunlavy, gdn (or Dunlevy)
Residence:	
Bound to:	Silas M. Cory/Corey Trade: tanner & currier
Residence:	WR Co.
Term:	until 21; 3Y & 3weeks
Witnesses:	A. H. Dunlevy & Joseph Monger

Page & date:	pp. 123-125 30 July 1829
Indentured:	Hiram Pugh
Age:	18Y 1M
Residence:	Montgomery Co.
Parent, guardian or officials:	-son of Benj. Pugh
Residence:	Montgomery Co.
Bound to:	John McGinness Trade: clothier & carder
Residence:	WR Co.
Term:	until 21 on 30 Jan 1832
Witnesses:	George C. & Mary Ward

Page & date:	pp. 125-126 13 Oct 1829
Indentured:	Daniel L. Stewart
Age:	10Y 4M 14D
Residence:	WR Co.
Parent, guardian or officials:	-son of William Stewart
Residence:	WR Co.
Bound to:	Josiah H. Bispham Trade: farming
Residence:	WR Co.
Term:	until 16 on 29 May 1835
Witnesses:	George C. Ward & Ner Haines

Page & date: p. 127   15 Sep 1829

Indentured: Francis Whitacre - previous indunture being
                                     voided; see pp. 113-114
Age: none given

Residence:

Parent, guardian -Samuel Nixon, gdn
or officials:

Residence:

Bound to: James M. Fisher   Trade: saddle & harnis
                                                           making
Residence: Lebanon

Term:

Witnesses: James Dunham(?)

Page & date: pp. 127-129   17 Oct 1829

Indentured: Aaron Taffe(?)

Age: will be 21 on 14 June 1833

Residence: WR Co.

Parent, guardian -Samuel Gustin, gdn
or officials:

Residence: WR Co.

Bound to: John Martin   Trade: laying brick

Residence:

Term: until 21

Witnesses: Jacoby Hallack

Page & date: pp. 129-130   29 Aug 1829

Indentured: Asa Harper

Age: 14Y 40D

Residence:

Parent, guardian -John James, gdn
or officials:

Residence:

Bound to: Francis B. Howell   Trade: paper making

Residence: WR Co.

Term: until 21 on 20 July 1836

Witnesses: John M. Seely

WARREN COUNTY, OHIO APPRENTICESHIP & INDENTURE RECORDS

Page & date: pp. 130-132   16 Oct 1829

Indentured: William Franklin Jacobs, a poor, destitute orphan
Age: 5Y old on 22 July 1829   child

Residence: Union Twp., WR Co.

Parent, guardian   -David Randolph, Jacob Doan & James T. Scott,J.P.
or officials: Trustees of Union Twp.

Residence: Union Twp.

Bound to: Jacob D. Lowe & Francis   Trade: farming
Residence: Union Twp.   his wife

Term: until 21 on 22 July 1845

Witnesses: Joab Snook & Adam Simonton

Page & date: pp. 132-133   16 Oct 1829

Indentured: Lucinda Matilda Jacobs, a poor, destitute orphan
Age: 4Y old on 22 Oct 1829   child

Residence: Union Twp.

Parent, guardian   -same officials as above
or officials:

Residence: Union Twp.

Bound to: same as above   Trade: housekeeping
Residence: Union Twp.

Term: until 18 on 22 Oct 1843

Witnesses: same as above

Page & date: pp. 133-135   3 Oct 1829

Indentured: Francis Whitacre
Age: 14Y 3M

Residence:

Parent, guardian   -Samuel Nixon, gdn
or officials:

Residence: WR Co.

Bound to: William Wood   Trade: carding & spinning
Residence: Lebanon   wool

Term: until 21 on 1 Oct 1836

Witnesses: W. Sellers

Page & date: pp. 135-136   28 Aug 1829

Indentured: Matilda Vance

Age: 1Y 7M 8D

Residence: WR Co.

Parent, guardian   -infant dau. of Joseph Vance
or officials:

Residence: WR Co.

Bound to: James & Anna Bennett   Trade: housekeeping

Residence:

Term: 16Y 4M 16D; until 18 on 8 Jan 1846

Witnesses: Isaac Gaskill

Page & date: pp. 136-137   24 Oct 1829

Indentured: William Brandon

Age: 17Y 4M 2D

Residence: WR Co.

Parent, guardian   -son of Absalom Brandon
or officials:

Residence: WR Co.

Bound to: Job Barton   Trade: taylor

Residence: WR Co.

Term: until 21 on 22 June 1833

Witnesses: Joseph H. Gilpin & William Stewart

Page & date: pp. 138-139   28 Aug 1829

Indentured: Mary Ann Eddington, a base(?) born child

Age: 9Y 1M 4D

Residence: WR Co.

Parent, guardian   -dau. of Margaret Bishir, wife of John Lecans(?);
or officials: dau. of W. Eddington

Residence: WR Co.

Bound to: David Odor   Trade: housekeeping

Residence: Cincinnati, OH

Term: 8Y 10M 26D; until 18 on 28 July 1838

Witnesses: Aaron Vanpelt & William N. Kirkwood

Page & date:	pp. 139-141 21 Nov 1829
Indentured:	Joseph Nickleson
Age:	19Y 1M 1D
Residence:	Washington Twp.
Parent, guardian or officials:	-son of Elizabeth Nickleson
Residence:	Washington Twp.
Bound to:	John Kesler/Keslar Trade: farming
Residence:	Salem Twp.
Term:	1Y 10M 30D
Witnesses:	Samuel & Emily Bowman; Westley & Lydia White

Page & date:	pp. 141-143 26 Nov 1829
Indentured:	David Stewart
Age:	8Y 2M 27D
Residence:	WR Co.
Parent, guardian or officials:	-son of William Stewart
Residence:	WR Co.
Bound to:	Daniel Haines Trade: farmer
Residence:	
Term:	until 21 on 29 Aug 1841
Witnesses:	George C. Ward

Page & date:	pp. 143-145 24 Nov 1829
Indentured:	Jacob Bowser
Age:	17Y 10M 4D
Residence:	Turtlecreek Twp.
Parent, guardian or officials:	-William H. Hamilton, gdn
Residence:	
Bound to:	Joseph Foote/Foot Trade: shoemaker
Residence:	Turtlecreek Twp.
Term:	3Y 1M 26D; until 21 on 20 Jan 1833
Witnesses:	Jacob Morris(?) & Francis Dunlevy

Page & date: pp. 145-146   28 Jan 1830

Indentured: Henry W. Ingersoll

Age: 15Y 11M 3D

Residence: Hamilton Twp.

Parent, guardian   -son of Benj Ingersoll
or officials:

Residence: Hamilton Twp.

Bound to: Frederic Snider   Trade: cabinet maker

Residence: Hamilton Twp.

Term: 4Y 22D

Witnesses: Robert Wilson & James Hopkins

Page & date: pp. 146-148   24 Apr 1830

Indentured: Jacob Egbert

Age: 16Y 3M 22D   as of 8 Mar

Residence: WR Co.

Parent, guardian   -son of Rachael Egbert, widow of John Egbert
or officials:

Residence: WR Co.

Bound to: William Bretney   Trade: saddling & harness
                                                    making
Residence: WR Co.

Term: 4Y commencing 8 Mar 1830; for 4Y until aged
                    20Y 3M 22D
Witnesses: A. H. Dunlevy

Page & date: pp. 148-149   28 Apr 1830

Indentured: Mirza F. Payne (male)

Age: 14Y 28D

Residence: WR Co.

Parent, guardian   -Gilbert Thompson, gdn
or officials:

Residence: WR Co.

Bound to: Tobias Bretney   Trade: tanning & currying

Residence: WR Co.

Term: 6Y 11M 2D; until 21 on 1 Apr 1837

Witnesses: J. M. Houston

Page & date:	pp. 149-151 20 Mar 1830
Indentured:	Spencer Vance
Age:	11Y 6M 14D
Residence:	Turtlecreek Twp.
Parent, guardian or officials:	-son of Joseph Vance
Residence:	Turtlecreek Twp.
Bound to:	James H. Corwin Trade: farmer
Residence:	Turtlecreek Twp.
Term:	9Y until 20 Mar 1839 when he will be 20½
Witnesses:	A. H. Dunlevy

Page & date:	pp. 151-152 10 Apr 1830
Indentured:	James Mix, a poor boy
Age:	10Y 5M
Residence:	probably Union Twp.
Parent, guardian or officials:	-David Randolph, John L. Armstrong & James T. Scott, Trustees of Union Twp.
Residence:	
Bound to:	Jesse Simson/Simpson Trade: weaver
Residence:	Union Twp.
Term:	9Y 7M until age 20 "...believe will happen...on 10 Nov 1839..."
Witnesses:	John Waldron & Joseph Smithers

Page & date:	pp. 153-154 10 June 1830
Indentured:	Samuel Hood
Age:	16Y on 15 Oct 1829
Residence:	probably Wayne Twp.
Parent, guardian or officials:	-Stephen Cover & Abnah Oneal, Trustees of Wayne Twp. Ellis Stokes, J.P.
Residence:	Wayne Twp.
Bound to:	Samuel Hartley Trade: blacksmithing
Residence:	Wayne Twp.
Term:	until 21 on 15 Oct 1834
Witnesses:	Ellis Stokes & Horace M. Stokes

Page & date:	pp. 155-156 23 June 1830
Indentured:	Joseph Stevenson
Age:	18Y 2M 10D
Residence:	WR Co.
Parent, guardian or officials:	-son of Samuel Stevenson
Residence:	WR Co.
Bound to:	Joel Satterthwaite Trade: waggon maker
Residence:	WR Co.
Term:	until 21 on 13 Apr 1833
Witnesses:	George C. & Mary Ward

Page & date:	pp. 156-157 2 Oct 1830
Indentured:	Jonathan Stephenson, a minor
Age:	16Y 1M 29D
Residence:	
Parent, guardian or officials:	-James Stephenson, gdn
Residence:	
Bound to:	Anthony Warwick Trade: blacksmithing
Residence:	Lebanon
Term:	until 21 on 2 Oct 1834
Witnesses:	Linus Williams & Joseph Koogle

Page & date:	p. 158 18 Sep 1828
Indentured:	Maria Lemmon
Age:	aged 4Y on this date
Residence:	WR Co.
Parent, guardian or officials:	-dau. of Pompey Lemmon
Residence:	WR Co.
Bound to:	Edward Smith Trade: housekeeping
Residence:	WR Do.
Term:	14Y; until 18
Witnesses:	Thos Corwin

Page & date:	pp. 158-160 4 Dec 1830
Indentured:	David Stewart
Age:	9Y 3M 5D
Residence:	WR Co.
Parent, guardian or officials:	-son of William Stewart
Residence:	WR Co.
Bound to:	Abraham Hawkins Trade: farmer
Residence:	WR Co.
Term:	until 21 on 29 Aug 1842
Witnesses:	George C. Ward

Page & date:	pp. 160-161 15 Oct 1830
Indentured:	James Watson, Jr.
Age:	17Y 11M 2D
Residence:	Turtlecreek Twp.
Parent, guardian or officials:	-son of James Watson
Residence:	Turtlecreek Twp.
Bound to:	Henry B. Miller Trade: cabinet maker
Residence:	Turtlecreek Twp.
Term:	3Y _M 2D; until 21 on 13 Nov 1833
Witnesses:	John Hathaway, Andrew McIlvain & Mason Lawless

Page & date:	pp. 161-163 27 Dec 1830
Indentured:	Joseph W. Johnson
Age:	15Y 1M 15D
Residence:	Turtlecreek Twp.
Parent, guardian or officials:	-son of Joseph J. Johnson, deceased; Joseph Foot, gdn
Residence:	Turtlecreek Twp.
Bound to:	Thomas Biggs Trade: saddler
Residence:	Turtlecreek Twp.
Term:	5Y 10M 15D; until 21 on 12 Nov 1836
Witnesses:	John B. Hose(?) & William Koogle

WARREN COUNTY, OHIO APPRENTICESHIP & INDENTURE RECORDS

Page & date:	pp. 163-165 18 Dec 1830
Indentured:	Elmore Meeks, a poor boy
Age:	18Y 9M 13D
Residence:	Hamilton Twp.
Parent, guardian or officials:	-son of Cath. Meeks, formerly of said twp who is unable to support her said child; John Hart & John Snook, overseers of the poor; Robert Wilson,
Residence:	J.P. - all of Hamilton Twp.
Bound to:	William Willison Trade: weaving
Residence:	Hamilton Twp.
Term:	until 21 "...believe will happen..." 5 Mar 1842; 12Y 2M 17D
Witnesses:	none

Page & date:	pp. 165-166 7 Dec 1830
Indentured:	David Edward Meek, a poor boy
Age:	7Y 1M
Residence:	probably Union Twp.
Parent, guardian or officials:	-James T. Scott & John L. Armstrong, Union Twp. Trustees
Residence:	
Bound to:	Edward D. Grigg Trade: farmer
Residence:	Union Twp.
Term:	13Y 11M; until 21 "...believe will happen..." on 7 Nov 1844
Witnesses:	none

Page & date:	pp. 166-168 3 Jan 1831
Indentured:	Abraham Davis Williams
Age:	17Y 3M 27D
Residence:	Wayne Twp.
Parent, guardian or officials:	-son of Israel Williams
Residence:	Wayne Twp.
Bound to:	Joseph McCawley Trade: taylor
Residence:	Wayne Twp.
Term:	3Y 8M 3D; until 21 on 7 Sep 1834
Witnesses:	Dennis Hopkins & Samuel Pike

WARREN COUNTY, OHIO APPRENTICESHIP & INDENTURE RECORDS

Page & date:	pp. 168-169 3 Jan 1831
Indentured:	Josiah P. Williams
Age:	15Y 2M 27D
Residence:	Wayne Twp.
Parent, guardian or officials:	- son of Israel Williams
Residence:	Wayne Twp.
Bound to:	George & Letitia Stip or Trade: farmer
Residence:	Sugar Creek Twp., Stipp Greene Co.
Term:	5Y 9M 27D until 21 on 30 Oct 1836
Witnesses:	John M. Hadden & Ishmael Pugh

Page & date:	pp. 169-171 1 Dec 1830
Indentured:	Nathaniel Foster (note: one of the signers of this indenture was William N Foster)
Age:	9Y 10M 10D
Residence:	Turtle Creek Twp.
Parent, guardian or officials:	-son of Cath Stanton
Residence:	Turtle Creek Twp.
Bound to:	Anthony Warwick Trade: blacksmith
Residence:	Turtle Creek Twp.
Term:	11Y 2M 20D; until 21 on 10 Feb 1842
Witnesses:	John Stanton & Benj. Blackburn

Page & date:	pp. 171-172 8 Dec 1830
Indentured:	Phebe Foster
Age:	11Y 11M 22D
Residence:	Turtle Creek Twp.
Parent, guardian or officials:	-dau. of Cath Stanton
Residence:	Turtle Creek Twp.
Bound to:	David Tullis Trade:
Residence:	Turtle Creek Twp.
Term:	6Y _M 8D; until 18 on 16 Dec 1836
Witnesses:	Israel Brandenburg & Benj. Blackburn

Page & date:	pp. 172-174 1 Oct 1830
Indentured:	Oliver Hester
Age:	16Y 5M 11D
Residence:	Wayne Twp.
Parent, guardian or officials:	-Stephen Covert & Obijah Oneal, overseers of the poor of Wayne Twp.; Ellis Stokes, J.P.
Residence:	
Bound to:	Joel Satterthwaite Trade: waggon maker
Residence:	Wayne Twp.
Term:	until 21 on 20 Apr 1835
Witnesses:	Ellis Stokes & Horace M. Stokes

Page & date:	pp. 174-175 2 Mar 1831
Indentured:	Silas Wood
Age:	14Y 2M
Residence:	
Parent, guardian or officials:	-Wyllys Pierson, gdn
Residence:	
Bound to:	James M. Fisher Trade: saddle & harnis making
Residence:	Lebanon
Term:	6Y 10M; until 21 on 1 Jan 1838
Witnesses:	Price Whitacre & Samuel Nixon

Page & date:	pp. 175-176 4 Apr 1831
Indentured:	Owen Jones
Age:	17Y 25D
Residence:	Wayne Twp.
Parent, guardian or officials:	-son of Jesse O. Jones
Residence:	Wayne Twp.
Bound to:	Job Borton Trade: tailor
Residence:	
Term:	3Y 11M 6D; until 21 on 10 Mar 1835
Witnesses:	James Watson & Benj. J. Pugh

Page & date: pp. 176-177   24 Jan 1831

Indentured: <u>William B. Davis</u>

Age: 16Y 11M 20D

Residence:

Parent, guardian -son of George Davis, deceased; Silas Hurin(?),
or officials: gdn

Residence: Butler Co., OH

Bound to: John B. Drake   Trade: saddler

Residence: Lebanon

Term: 4y 10D; until 21 on 4 Feb 1835

Witnesses: A. Vannote & Thomas Shearman

Page & date: pp. 178-179   21 Mar 1831

Indentured: <u>John Cummins</u>

Age: 15Y 11M 25D

Residence:

Parent, guardian -William Cummins, gdn.
or officials:

Residence:

Bound to: Lewis Osborn   Trade: tanner & currier

Residence:

Term: 5Y 5D; until 21 on 26 Mar 1836

Witnesses: Thomas Seaman

Page & date: pp. 179-180   6 June 1831

Indentured: <u>Ferman (or Fermen) Snook</u>

Age: 16Y

Residence: Union Twp.

Parent, guardian -son of John M. Snook
or officials:

Residence: Union Twp.

Bound to: Asbury Frazier   Trade: tailoring

Residence: Turtle Creek Twp.

Term: 4Y; until 20 on 6 June 1835

Witnesses: W. Sellers

Page & date: pp. 180-181   25 May 1831

Indentured: Joseph Garard or Garrard

Age: 17Y 9M 12D

Residence: Turtle Creek Twp.

Parent, guardian   -son of John Garrard/Garard
or officials:

Residence:

Bound to: Henry B. Miller   Trade: cabinet making

Residence: Turtle Creek Twp.

Term: 3Y; until 25 May 1834 when "...Joseph Garrard will
                         be under twenty years of age..."

Witnesses: J. A. J. Blair & S. Hurin(?)

Page & date: p. 182   23 Apr 1831

Indentured: Daniel S. Stewart

Age: 11Y 10M 24D

Residence: Wayne Twp.

Parent, guardian   -son of William Stewart
or officials:

Residence: Wayne Twp.

Bound to: Jason Evans   Trade: farmer

Residence: Wayne Twp.

Term: 9Y 1M 6D; until 21 on 29 May 1840

Witnesses: Ellis Stokes & William Small

Page & date: pp. 183-184   1 July 1831

Indentured: John Pearson

Age: will be 8Y old on 24 Feb. next (1832)

Residence:

Parent, guardian   -son of John Pearson
or officials:

Residence: WR Co.

Bound to: John Martin   Trade: not stated

Residence:

Term: until 21

Witnesses: Noah Wheeler & Charles Thomson

Page & date: pp. 183-184   1 July 1831

Indentured: <u>Mahlon Pearson</u>

Age: will be 7Y on 19 March next (1832)

Residence:

Parent, guardian -son of John Pearson
or officials:

Residence: WR Co.

Bound to: John Martin   Trade: not stated

Residence:

Term: until 21

Witnesses: Noah Wheeler & Charles Thomson

Page & date: pp. 183-184   1 July 1831

Indentured: <u>James Pearson</u>

Age: will be 6Y on 19 May next (1832)

Residence:

Parent, guardian -son of John Pearson
or officials:

Residence: WR Co.

Bound to: John Martin   Trade: not stated

Residence:

Term: until 21

Witnesses: Noah Wheeler & Charles Thomson

Page & date: pp. 184-185   12 May 1831

Indentured: <u>Lucinda Layfollett</u>, a poor girl

Age: 8Y 2M 17D

Residence: Hamilton Twp.

Parent, guardian -John Snook & John Hart, overseers of the poor,
or officials: Hamilton Twp.; Robert Wilson, J.P.; dau. of Sarah
Layfolette - who is unable to support her child
Residence: Hamilton Twp.

Bound to: Swanson L. Griffith   Trade: housewife

Residence: Hamilton Twp.

Term: 9Y 10M 8D; until 18 on 25 Feb 1841

Witnesses: F. U. Snider(?) & Joseph H. Johnson

Page & date: pp. 185-186   16 Apr 1831

Indentured: David A. Smith

Age: none given

Residence:

Parent, guardian - son of John Smith
or officials:

Residence:

Bound to: F. B. Howell   Trade: paper making

Residence: WR Co.

Term: until 1 Dec. 1832 (probably when 21, but not
                         so stated)

Witnesses: Samuel Hannan & H. Brown

Page & date: pp. 187-188   5 Mar 1831

Indentured: David Parent

Age: 16Y

Residence: Turtle Creek Twp.

Parent, guardian -with consent of his father (not named, but
or officials: probably Hiram Parent, one of the signers)

Residence:

Bound to: F. B. Howell   Trade: paper maker

Residence: Turtle Creek Twp.

Term: 5Y; until 21 on 5 Mar 1836

Witnesses: James Snider

Page & date: pp. 188-190   7 Mar 1831

Indentured: Samuel Turner, a poor boy

Age: 5Y (11M scratched out) 13D

Residence: probably Salem Twp.

Parent, guardian -Wm Arnstrong, Lewis Sever & Wm Crosson, J.P. -
or officials: Trustees of Salem Twp.; son of Sarah Daughman who
Residence: is unable to support her said child

Bound to: Edward C. Johnston   Trade: farmer

Residence: Salem Twp.

Term: 16Y 17D; until 21 on 24 March(?) 1847

Witnesses: Wm Patterson & David H. Smith

Page & date:	pp. 190-191 5 Sep 1831
Indentured:	Benj. Fithen or Fithian
Age:	17Y 4M 5D
Residence:	Green Twp., Clark Co.
Parent, guardian or officials:	-son of Israel Fithian
Residence:	Green Twp., Clark Co.
Bound to:	David Baker Trade: tailor
Residence:	Turtle Creek Twp.
Term:	3Y 7M 25D; until 21 on 1 May 1835
Witnesses:	Benj. Blackburn & Wm Smith

Page & date:	pp. 191-192 3 Sep 1831
Indentured:	Archibald Cary
Age:	18Y
Residence:	Wayne Twp.
Parent, guardian or officials:	-son of Hannah Cary
Residence:	Wayne Twp.
Bound to:	Joseph McCawly Trade: tailor
Residence:	Wayne Twp.
Term:	3Y; until 21 on 3 Sep 1834
Witnesses:	David Harvey & Thomas Moore

Page & date:	pp. 192-193 3 Sep 1831
Indentured:	Henry Bingamin
Age:	15Y 11M 1D
Residence:	
Parent, guardian or officials:	-son of Lewis Bingamin
Residence:	Sugar Creek Twp., Greene Co., OH
Bound to:	Stephen Covert Trade: wheelright
Residence:	Wayne Twp.
Term:	4Y 3M 29D; until aged 20Y 2M 29D on 3 Jan 1836
Witnesses:	Ellis Stokes & Horace M.(?) Stokes

Page & date:	pp. 194-195 11 June 1831
Indentured:	Benj. S. Rue, a poor boy
Age:	14Y 4M 17D
Residence:	
Parent, guardian or officials:	-James Cowan, James Frazier & Benj. Blackburn, Trustees of Turtle Creek Twp.; Wm Sellers, J.P.
Residence:	
Bound to:	Richard Parcell, Jr. Trade: tinner
Residence:	Turtle Creek Twp.
Term:	6Y 7M 13D; until 21 on 25 Jan 1838
Witnesses:	Jesse B. Corwin & A. Geoghegan

Page & date:	pp. 195-197 11 Oct 1831
Indentured:	Owen Jones
Age:	17Y 6M 1D
Residence:	
Parent, guardian or officials:	-son of Jesse O. Jones
Residence:	Wayne Twp.
Bound to:	Benj. Kemp Trade: tailor
Residence:	Wayne Twp.
Term:	3Y 6M; until 21 on 10 Mar 1835
Witnesses:	Micajah Johnson & Joshua Edwards

Page & date:	pp. 197-198 10 Oct 1831
Indentured:	Martha Ann Carzard or Carzart or Carzad
Age:	7Y 10M (a female)
Residence:	
Parent, guardian or officials:	-dau. of Orphey or Orphy Carzad
Residence:	Wayne Twp.
Bound to:	Joseph H. Burgess & Mary Trade: not stated
	his wife
Residence:	WR Co.
Term:	until 18
Witnesses:	John T. Burgess & Tacy Burgess

Page & date:	pp. 198-199 19 Aug 1831
Indentured:	William McKinney
Age:	12Y 4M 13D
Residence:	
Parent, guardian or officials:	-son of Lewis McKinney
Residence:	Wayne Twp.
Bound to:	Joseph H. Burgess Trade: tanner & currier of leather
Residence:	Wayne Twp.
Term:	8Y 7M 2weeks
Witnesses:	Simon D. Harvey & Thomas M. Wales

Page & date:	pp. 199-201 29 Oct 1831
Indentured:	William H. Baty or Beaty
Age:	12Y 6M (indenture cancelled 7 Oct 1834)
Residence:	
Parent, guardian or officials:	-son of Clarrissa Baty; Daniel Voorhis, gdn.
Residence:	Union Twp.
Bound to:	Lewis Chamberlan or Chamberlain Trade: waggonmaker
Residence:	Turtle (Creek) Twp.
Term:	8Y; until aged 20Y 6M on 29 Oct 1839
Witnesses:	Benj. Blackburn & A. F. Neal

Page & date:	pp. 201-203 16 Jan 1832
Indentured:	Jesse Jones (he left Chamberlin, indenture voided 8 Feb 1834, wit - Edward B. Wright)
Age:	16Y
Residence:	Turtle Creek Twp.
Parent, guardian or officials:	-son of Joseph Jones
Residence:	
Bound to:	Lewis Chamberlin Trade: waggon maker
Residence:	Turtle Creek Twp.
Term:	4Y; until 20 on 16 Jan 1836
Witnesses:	Joshua Soule(?), Jr. & W. Sellers

Page & date:	pp. 203-205 31 Mar 1864 (jumps from 1832 to 1864)
Indentured:	Ida Virginia Burch
Age:	1Y on 12 Aug 1863
Residence:	Union Village
Parent, guardian or officials:	-Amanda Bowser, alias Burch, of Clermont Co., bound her infant child
Residence:	Union Village (?)
Bound to:	Olivar C. Hampton Trade:
Residence:	Union Village, WR Co. (a member of the United Society of Believers Community called Shakers at Union Village)
Term:	until 18
Witnesses:	Thomas J. Embree

Page & date:	pp. 205-206 23 Apr 1864
Indentured:	Charles E. Bassett
Age:	4Y on 11 Mar 1864
Residence:	
Parent, guardian or officials:	-son of Mary Bassett
Residence:	Hamilton Co., OH
Bound to:	Oliver C. Hampton Trade: farmer
Residence:	Union Village (see above)
Term:	until 21 on 11 Mar 1881
Witnesses:	Thomas J. Embrose & Moses Miller(?)

Page & date:	pp. 206-208 31 May 1866
Indentured:	Sallie Randall
Age:	not given (12 years old ?)
Residence:	
Parent, guardian or officials:	-R.S. Lockwood, gdn
Residence:	WR Co.
Bound to:	Oliver Hampton Trade: housework
Residence:	Union Village (see above)
Term:	
Witnesses:	

WARREN COUNTY, OHIO APPRENTICESHIP & INDENTURE RECORDS

Page & date: pp. 208-210   1866

Indentured: John Myers

Age: 11Y on 2 Feb (1866 ?)

Residence:

Parent, guardian -John H. Reickel, gdn
or officials:

Residence: WR Co.

Bound to: Oliver Hampton   Trade: gardener

Residence: Union Village (see above)

Term: until 21 on 2 Feb 1876

Witnesses: Maria Wheeler

Page & date: pp. 210-212   1 Feb 1867

Indentured: William J. Bell

Age: 9Y on 27 Oct 1866

Residence: WR Co.

Parent, guardian -Aaron Stephens, Abraham Brant & John Drake,
or officials: Infirmary Commissioners of WR Co.

Residence:

Bound to: Oliver Hampton   Trade: gardener

Residence: Union Village (see above)

Term: until 21

Witnesses: Daniel Miller & E. J. Tichenor(?)

Page & date: pp. 212-214   1 Feb 1867

Indentured: William Morris

Age: none given

Residence: WR Co.

Parent, guardian -same officials as above
or officials:

Residence:

Bound to: Olvier Hampton   Trade: farmer

Residence: Union Village (see above)

Term: until 21

Witnesses: same as previous indenture

INDEX TO INDENTURED CHILDREN

INDEX TO INDENTURED CHILDREN

INDEX TO INDENTURED CHILDREN

www.ingramcontent.com/pod-product-compliance
Lightning Source LLC
Chambersburg PA
CBHW060642280326
41933CB00012B/2117